SUMMER WINE
Country

PAVILION
MICHAEL JOSEPH

SUMMER WINE
Country

ROY CLARKE

PHOTOGRAPHS BY
PAUL BARKER

First published in 1989 by
PAVILION BOOKS LIMITED
196 Shaftesbury Avenue, London WC2H 8JL
in association with Michael Joseph Limited
27 Wrights Lane, London, W5 8TZ

Text copyright © Roy Clarke 1989
Photographs copyright © Paul Barker 1989
Map by David Williams © Pavilion Books 1989

Designed by Roger Daniels, Peartree Design Associates

A CIP catalogue record for this book is
available from the British Library.

ISBN 1 85145 412 8

10 9 8 7 6 5 4 3 2 1

Printed and bound by Mohndruck, West Germany

Summer Wine Country

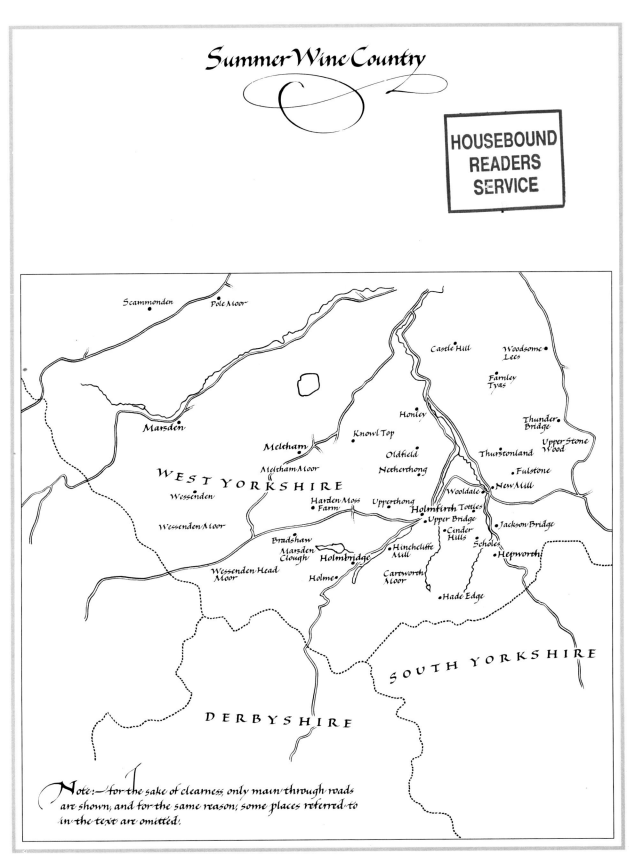

Note:— for the sake of clearness, only main through roads are shown, and for the same reason, some places referred to in the text are omitted.

INTRODUCTION

THE FOLLOWING IS AN extract from letters written by Norman Clegg of this parish to his Polish penfriend Tad. Tad is, of course, an abbreviation for something much longer but Tad was as far as Clegg felt able to go.

Clegg asks me to provide a word of explanation regarding the reasons for his uncharacteristic

followers of the late Josiah H Ormeroyd, a rich platitude manufacturer with a vision of international harmony. The two neo-Bloomsbury ladies who had just run over Clegg lost no time in trying to co-opt him for the cause. He had just enough breath left to resist actually becoming a member

opening up of communications of a Polish nature. It was not, he wishes to make clear, his own idea. Left to his own devices he would have felt absolutely no need, he assures me, to inflict himself upon a nation with enough trouble to be going on with. What happened was he was knocked down by the Ormeroyd Society. Two of them, on bicycles, caught him as he was crossing Upper Hebden Street with his nose buried in the evening paper.

The Ormeroyd Society is a group of dedicated (some would say impossible)

but was shaken enough to find himself agreeing to an assignment on an *ad hoc* basis. He was given Tad's name and address and it was winter and he had the long nights to fill, and thus began his contact with a corner of Eastern Europe and a Polish thirst for knowledge of Clegg's Yorkshire which he was immensely relieved to find was not of a military nature.

In these letters, Clegg sought to give his Polish friend some idea of the 'feel' of his birthplace and its surroundings. Let Clegg then introduce us to *Summer Wine Country*.

Dear Tad,

Where do I come from you ask. I used to see my father looking at me and wondering exactly the same thing. He was a native here. My mother also. As were their families for generations. That was the pattern then. To be here meant, almost certainly, that you were born here. These were small communities confined by harsh winters to their own valleys.

We are a hill people. It's not the Himalayas. We don't go in for such drama. We haven't even a small mountain, nevertheless the sides of our valleys are often steep. Up and down is our way of life. Gravity has a reality, hereabouts, unknown on the flat. It gives us, we believe, a touch more weight in our characters.

We live in an area of great natural beauty but this is no land for lotus eaters. It's a good day round here when you don't need a pullover. My generation anyway. We were raised to heavy clothing. It was a time when faith in the sturdiest garments went unquestioned. Some of us date the moral decline from the abandoning of the woolly vest. This respect the elders have for substantial clothing is perhaps the thing which separates us most clearly from our young. We see the generation gap personified in those few inches of young flesh forever gaping between their T-shirts and their jeans. Inches, often, of goose-pimpled flesh. The quest to ape California fashions is not always a happy one round here.

Whatever the fads of adolescent fashions, sturdy clothing is more typical of my generation. It's the equivalent on our backs of the durability of our houses. We build in stone. The grey local stone which weathers and blends our dwellings into the hillsides as if they've grown there.

Being small communities we fit acceptably into our landscape. We have the happiness to have the balance right. Everywhere the landscape dominates us. We have not (yet) overwhelmed it. The sheer inconvenience of our hills has kept the despoilers at bay.

Perhaps it's to this stubborn example of the hills that we owe our own obstinacy. Non-conformism runs strongly in us. We have plain but proud tastes and can judge expertly brass bands, great choral societies and cricket.

As I said we have no mountains but we are the kind of people who would be unimpressed by mountains on the grounds that you can't really do much with them. Ornament alone, hereabouts, is insufficient. We are programmed for utility. We use our hills. Sheep graze the high moors and wherever we can grow it we sow grass and enclose it with dry stone walls. There's an old craft; walls without mortar which, nevertheless, withstand our winds and even our centuries.

We have had the enormous blessing of being left for so long in peace. Except by the tourists we haven't been invaded since the eleventh century. We were never much for excitement. Poor old Poland has had more than her share. How you

SLAITHWAITE MOOR

must have resented those arrogant intruders. I know we would.

But that's the big picture. If you wish to know, as you say, what my life is like we need the smaller scale. My days, for all their freedom, have an iron ring of habit. I wake up in a bedroom which is just as it was when my wife was alive. It's in the style which she achieved so apparently effortlessly in all things, and which was second nature to her – Yorkshire Respectable. The rule is absolutely nothing flash. The wardrobe is mahogany and the matching dressing-table contains her toilet set (it was a wedding present). She used to clean it rather than use it. Her generation were wary of perfume. They called it scent. Hers has long since evaporated, though funnily enough, I can always still smell it – especially at nights.

The bathroom's not changed much either. Everything white. Like bathrooms used to be. The original cast-iron bath. No form of heating – again like bathrooms used to be. You begin to see what I mean about heavy clothing. Some people round here even get washed wearing a cardigan. But that's us oldies. The young, like the young everywhere, are all coloured suites and central heating. Things which coincided with their time, if not ours, luckily for them or think what a brake could have been put on their sexual revolution.

I still wet-shave. I tried an electric once but it cut me. I couldn't believe it. There I was cutting my throat – and with an electric razor.

I'm compulsive about breakfast. I probably drink too much tea. Everything we've always liked seems to be turning out to be bad for us. But I still mash mine in a stoneware pot and the first cup gets me going. I like a good breakfast and something solid enough to counterbalance the general gloom of the morning papers. I usually manage to remain undepressed. I'm old enough to be unimpressed by the papers. There has to be something of a cheat about all the news in the world managing to fit itself neatly every morning into the same number of pages.

When I step outside to fetch the milk in I see a row of stone houses, very similar to mine and I see roofs below me and beyond these, the countryside. When the wind's right I can smell the moors. On my own doorstep I can smell the moors.

Downhill I can hear the traffic of the town. Too much of it as everywhere these days. In places we still have cobblestones. We were built for the iron wheel and for the hoof.

As I descend to town down streets that I know, I pass houses I know containing people I know. It must be the same for you. It gives a solid context to our lives. If 'all the world's a stage' as a near Yorkshireman once said, for those of us with walk-on parts there's a lot of comfort to be had from all the other minor players.

Our town is unspectacular. Nothing showy. Yorkshire Respectable again. But it fits like a glove. And its great glory is all that countryside on its doorstep.

Most days, I join a couple of cronies and go walking. Out there sometimes in the silence of the hills you get to marvelling. At that long chain of evolution; at Nature's patient shaping through some billion years this marvel she lays at our feet.

Wishing you a life fit to live in and the chance to enjoy it in peace.

Yours Yorkshirely,

Norman Clegg

The snow's going. There's very little left even up the tops. I'm not suggesting there's any sign of Spring. It was cold up there and as we started moving down and saw the town it seemed to be under the wildest of winter skies. Could this be winter's last bluff and bluster? I asked the others. Seymour lectured me for five minutes on what he could remember of meteorology and what he couldn't remember I feel sure he made up. Compo came up with the definitive answer. Nora Batty is still wearing her thickest stockings. You can't argue against that. It's still winter.

*C*ousin Desmond's funeral. I had to go to Peterborough. It was a decent funeral but I felt like an outsider. About the only person I really knew was Cousin Desmond and he wasn't much help. Came back from Peterborough with a sense of relief. Peterborough is flat. I hadn't realised how flat flat is. You travel through the streets and all you see is the street. You don't see any roofs. Back home I realized how we live among roofs. You turn any corner and you're looking at roofs. I like living among roofs. It adds a dimension to your daily existence. I wonder if Cousin Desmond missed these roofs.

previous page
MARSDEN FROM POLE MOOR

left
HOLMFIRTH

overleaf
SHEEP ON SCAMMONDEN MOOR
AFTER HAILSTORM

13

Still some snow in the cracks and furrows of the high moor tops. We're a long way from the sea but we have landscapes of oceanic proportions. Up there you navigate with a sense of your own smallness. You feel the weight of the sky. You get dizzy on so much oxygen. You return to the inhabited world tired but exhilarated. You need time to wind down or suffer a kind of spiritual 'bends'. You reacclimatize gradually to the more limited horizons of the ordinary and the routine daily. Now as I write this here in my house it's dark outside. I can still feel the pleasant afterburn of wind on my cheek. These old legs are very conscious of the miles today and many of our miles, it has to be remembered, are worth more than two on the flat. I shall go to bed early. I have clean pyjamas warming near the fire. The kettle boiling; my slippers on. After that enormous world this morning I have a fondness for its cozy counterpart.

*W*e went way out this afternoon. It was enjoyable and warm. Then Raggy Britches decided he needed a drink of water. This in itself was something of an innovation. His connection to water being habitually somewhat slender. Seymour pointed out a trickle of spring water. 'I'm not drinking that.' Compo said with a sudden unconvincing caution with regard to germs. 'I want a mug.' Despite our qualms he called at a house. They very kindly gave him a glass. We were much relieved, having expected that the sight of him wandering down their path might have brought the shutters slamming and the drawbridge crashing up.

'*I* *should have been a farmer,' Compo said. 'You don't get up early enough,' Seymour pointed out. 'But I would do if I'd been a farmer,' Compo insisted. 'Farming is hard work,' Seymour said. 'I'm not afraid of . . .'. 'Don't lie.' Seymour interrupted. As we walked home we saw the farmer staggering under the weight of a sheep he was carrying. 'I should have been a Chartered Accountant,' Compo said.*

left
THURSTONLAND

below
BRADSHAW

We were walking. We were talking nonsense, which we do fluently. I was thinking about nothing profounder than what I might fancy for dinner when suddenly I was grabbed by an angle of the landscape which insisted that I stop and admire it. It was a summons I couldn't ignore. There is such power in arrangements of earth and sky and that which grows between. It can snatch you from idle things to demand respect. You find yourself in the grip of arguments which persuade without words. 'Get a move on', they said. 'What are you hanging back for?' 'Just catching my breath,' I said.

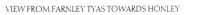

VIEW FROM FARNLEY TYAS TOWARDS HONLEY

We were out early today, to a lovely, bright morning with a keen frost. One of Spring's finest weather recipes. That touch of sharpness which stops things being too sweet for the palate. On average, about three days a week, I fall in love with trees. I'm a tree groupie. I fall for them in whole platoons or singly. I have no problem understanding why the ancients used to worship trees. When I hear the snarl of a chain saw I can still feel, persistent in the blood, a residue of blasphemy.

left
RUSHFIELD DIKE, WOODSOME

below
TREE NEAR CASTLE HILL

*W*hat will they make of us, I wonder, in centuries to come? From their glass and ceramic or their plastic palaces how will they view our world of stone? Will they reconstruct with any accuracy our dwellings set snugly among our folds and valleys? Will our stone appear to them as almost stone age? What will their archaeology construe of our culture? From our litter and the cans the trippers leave how will the future calculate our stubbornness, our York-shireness and our stony humour?

left
DERELICT FARM, CARTWORTH MOOR

above
FIELD AND TREES NEAR CASTLE HILL

overleaf
VIEW OF HOLME FROM CARTWORTH MOOR

We were up near Oggy's place this morning and the sky, as usual, was being enormous. It blows up there. It occurred to me that there can't be many days in a year when Oggy is not exposed to a draught. Perhaps this accounts for a certain crustiness in his nature which is difficult to penetrate. Oggy's in there somewhere but it's not always easy to tell. This is particularly noticeable when it's his turn to buy a round. Hints just bounce off that weatherbeaten exterior. Oggy's selective deafness is a thing of beauty. To see him and Seymour locked in non-spending combat is almost worth the dryness of the wait. I wonder if that's how chess got invented.

We're still getting frost in the mornings. The faintest dusting on the grass. The air's crisp enough to keep you walking. It builds an appetite. The robins were singing. We shared our sandwiches with Compo and the robins. Guess who got most although he can't sing a note.

HAGG COTTAGE, OLDFIELD

right
HORSE ON CARTWORTH MOOR
below
COWS AT WOODSOME LEES

We were stared at today as we passed some curious neighbours in their fields. They watched us with an interest as keen as human. You can't help thinking as you pass those not unfriendly faces that it's only the absence of some tiny key; some small adjustment we haven't yet tumbled to, that prevents us exchanging a 'Good morning' and entering into a few comments about the weather. We said 'Good morning' anyway. Why not?

We sat for a while up there today. It was pleasant in the sun. The other two were arguing from habit, almost reflexively. It made a kind of pleasant, droning background. I took one look at the view and had no wish to book a fortnight on the Costa anything.

VIEW FROM CARTWORTH MOOR TOWARDS
HOLME
overleaf
MEAL HILL FARM

*S*ometimes in our wanderings when we believe ourselves to be miles from any habitation we come across a dwelling in some wild location. Who builds we wonder way out there? Who was so desperate for solitude? Somebody must love the vastness of his daily view or he'd come scuttling back down to the shelter of the valleys and the complexities of people.

We climbed this morning to where the views were aerial. We took sandwiches and beer. I ate my lunch well back from the edge. 'Don't panic,' Seymour said. 'Fear of heights is all in the mind.' Seymour demonstrated his own fearlessness. 'If you think you're going to fall,' Seymour said, 'you're practically guaranteeing that you'll fall. But if you have confidence,' Seymour said. Then Seymour went quiet. When we looked up from our sandwiches we saw that the reason Seymour had gone quiet was that Seymour had gone. We could hear him slithering down the slope and calling something not very clearly but which didn't sound like a continuation of his lecture on fear of heights. It was Compo who recovered quickest from our surprise. 'I'll swap you one cheese for one ham,' Compo said. We made the exchange. 'What's Seymour having?' Compo asked. But Seymour had apparently taken his sandwiches with him. He reappeared after about fifteen minutes, his tie askew and his sleeve torn. He climbed wearily over the edge and glared at us balefully. We were stretched out comfortably having a post-luncheon nap. He didn't seem at all proud that we hadn't panicked.

VIEW OF BANK TOP FROM FIRTH PULE, MARSDEN

right
SHEEP FEEDING, ROODS LANE, HOLMEBRIDGE

below
THICK HOLLINS MOOR

*M*any animals have gentle eyes. Watched the news this evening and wished that might be true of humans. Up in the hills this morning we debated whether animals experience boredom. Compo claimed that they do and rolled up his trouser leg to show the scar where his ferret bit him. 'What,' Seymour wanted to know 'was it doing up his trouser leg in the first place?' Or even the second place. 'Boredom,' Compo said. 'Never would have gone up there if it hadn't been bored.' Seymour said he could sympathize with that but nothing was ever going to be that bored. A car passed us with the usual day trippers; a man and wife. They looked that bored. Homo sapiens at leisure seem to have a flair for being bored. The animals in the fields seem to eat most of the time. Maybe that's how they handle their boredom. 'Not so unlike somebody we both know.' Seymour said. 'Especially if you include beer as a food.' On the way home the sky darkened. We expected a storm but the sheep went on with their grazing. It didn't rain. They'd judged it better than we did.

We found a welly nest this morning. There it was inside an open doorway. Containing mother, father and two sets of twins. Compo says wellies are the world's most useful footwear. He attributes his consistently good health to the medical properties of wellies. 'It's the rubber,' Compo says. 'It insulates the wearer from bad electricity. It's bad electricity that causes diseases. It comes up through the ground.' Compo says. 'Those are moles,' Seymour said. It was Seymour, who later, reflecting upon how many windows the houses have round here, offered to organize the two of us into a window cleaning round. It's a good job Compo was wearing wellies. There were sparks about.

above
COTTAGE AT TOTTIES

left
WELLIES IN DOORWAY, OLDFIELD

*W*e half carried him home. When I say 'home' I mean to the nearest pub. He was sadly in need of refreshment. We lowered him very gently into a chair in the bar. There were tears in his eyes. 'Never again,' he swore. It sounded like a solemn vow. We watched him sink a pint with his usual facility. There was nothing wrong with that end. 'We warned you,' Seymour reminded him. 'I've done it a dozen times before,' Compo argued. 'When you were young and foolish instead of old and foolish,' Seymour grinned. Compo had tried to leapfrog one of the old stones.

above
WHITE HORSE INN, JACKSON BRIDGE

left
TENTER POSTS, MARSDEN

overleaf
RAKE DIKE, HOLME

A weasel,' Compo said. 'Where?' Seymour asked. 'In that stone wall,' Compo insisted. 'Just poked its head out.' There followed some argument about the exactness of the sighting. It was decided that we should wait quietly, staring at the wall, to see if the creature reappeared. It was a nice stone wall as stone walls go, but it was becoming apparent that I had only a limited concentration span for a stone wall. It didn't reappear. 'There was a weasel,' Compo said flatly. 'What would it be doing in a stone wall?' Seymour enquired. 'They live in stone walls,' Compo scoffed at Seymour's ignorance. 'Really,' Seymour said. 'Makes you wonder what they did before stone walls came along.' 'That's what animals are like,' Compo said. 'They make use of places.'

Young man in the pub today home on leave from a job in Saudi Arabia. He bought us a drink. Which seemed unfair to me. If anybody deserves having a drink bought it's somebody who works in Saudi Arabia. We asked him if he missed the greenery and he said he did. He's going back anyway. There are some sad cases around.

The thing about our town is how quickly we move from stone to greenery. Our streets are enclosed, and when the wind's not scuttling through them, almost cozy. Then we turn a corner or climb a rise and suddenly there's a world out there which goes forever. Although, admittedly, forever gets a bit smaller as you get older.

above
HOLMFIRTH

right
HEPWORTH

We took some bread cakes and a bit of butter and some cheese and ate them outdoors above the town. It tasted delicious. I don't know how many more taste points you could score with haute cuisine. And we had sparrows fussing about us and a chaffinch instead of waiters. I found the demeanour of the chaffinch to be infinitely more soothing than that of the waiter.

HOLMFIRTH

*W*ithout any conscious intention, we found ourselves, this morning, near the old barn where we used to play as lads. It was derelict even then. It's worse now. The roof's nearly all gone. We climbed through a hole in the wall less nimbly than we once did. It smelled the same as sixty years ago. That smell brought back a flood of memories. It was here Compo cut himself on his new penknife. Today he spat on his finger to clean it and showed us the scar. In this dangerous century England's been best for smaller scars.

DERELICT BARN, NETHERTHONG

overleaf
FULSTONE VIEW OF UPPER STONE WOOD

We were looking at the view. 'It makes you believe that there's something more awesome and powerful than man,' Seymour said. 'Nora Batty,' Compo said. We went to the pub. Compo has that ability to bring us down to earth. But it was still a nice view.

*W*e were sprawled comfortably above the little stream. They were asleep. They'd been arguing steadily but now they were asleep. Both snoring. I swear an argument to them is like a sedative. It simply puts them into a pleasant, drowsy mood. I could hear a curlew and a skylark and the snores. I went down to the stream. They didn't wake. The water was shallow and clear. There was an underwater world as clean as the morning of creation. As clean as the world was when it was handed to us, new. In showroom condition. Given to us with all its beauty and all its terrors. In that underwater world, in patches of sun or in green, weedy twilight I could see life darting about its urgent business; eating and being eaten. I stand there on a bridge, thinking we ourselves seem to be some kind of bridge between the beauty and the terror.

EASTER GATE, MARSDEN

*T*ook some flowers to the churchyard. It would have been her birthday. We were never very close. I never really knew what her dreams were – what she really liked. Although I know she liked flowers. Her name, carved in stone, is already beginning to weather. That same weathering has happened to me. I wonder if she'd recognize me. On the way home I suddenly saw how the years have remodelled Compo's features. And Time has tampered with Seymour's face. But we went to the pub and ignored all this – which is as it should be. Dates carved in stone are one thing, but lives are written in softer alphabets – transient but pleasant.

right
HOLMFIRTH

below
HOLME SUNDAY SCHOOL

We didn't go far today. Just far enough to enjoy the morning. And what a morning it was. The kind that makes you feel sorry for all who have to live in baked brown, arid countries. It can be cold and wet and miserable round here but when the sweet days come they come like nowhere else.

left
JACKSON BRIDGE

below
OLDFIELD ROAD

*S*uddenly realized how much stone surrounds us. Stone is a part of us here. It's not unfitting. We need a bit of it in our spirits if only to stiffen us for the winters. This should not be taken to mean that we are without affection for the softer things. We know how well stone is improved by daffodils. What a joy after winter's monochrome those explosions of colour.

right
DAFFODILS, NEW MILL

below
DIGLEY RESERVOIR

*T*here was a door-to-door salesman in the pub this lunchtime. A sadder and a wiser man, with his jacket off, mopping his brow. 'You earn your money round here,' he said. 'I've never seen so many steps. Your doors are all over the place. Why don't you have 'em on the level like anybody else?' 'What's tha' selling?' Compo asked. 'I'm selling damn all,' the salesman said. 'I climb the steps. I ring the bell. They open the door and I'm standing there gasping like a prawn. Before I can get me breath they've got the door shut again.'

'Tha wants to try Nora Batty's,' Compo said. 'I'll give thee her address. If tha rings her bell while she's busy – she'll speak to thee.'

above
NORA BATTY'S, HOLMFIRTH

left
HOLMFIRTH

overleaf
RAPESEED FIELD, HARTSHEAD

This morning Compo and Seymour were arguing the merits of education. 'I had some,' Seymour said, 'and I finished up as headmaster of my own school. You didn't bother with education and look where you ended up.'
'Right,' Compo agreed, 'and where did I end up?' Regular mates with a bloke who used to be headmaster of his own school.' Seymour went quiet. We passed a field of rape. There seems to be a plot afoot to turn the English countryside into a banana. Somebody ought to whisper that that little yellow flower has a bad case of B.O.

*M*et Sandford in town looking brown. He didn't seem to be doing anything except looking brown. While we were talking to him he kept making a great point of looking brown until finally Compo said, 'Hey up Sandford, tha's looking brown.' This enabled Sandford to relax his looking-brown muscles and he became once again the amiable idiot we all know and love. Turns out he's just back from a fortnight in some place where there wasn't a tree. Can you imagine paying money to go to places where there isn't a tree?

above
DEAN HEAD BANK, LITTLE CAKE

right
HEY GREEN, MARSDEN

*W*ashday – and the women are touchy. The town was busy with men keeping out of the way. You can spot them in the pubs and in the Pigeon Club and window shopping at the D.I.Y. store. They have that 'keeping out of the way' look in their eyes. They kill time until it's safe to go home. And it never is safe really, not on washday. It's only tomorrow that routines will be re-established and the women will be, once again, fit to talk to.

above
CHOPPARDS LANE

left
LYDGATE, NEW MILL

Seymour has taken up painting. Which means that Compo and I have taken up helping Seymour carry all the clobber an artist of Seymour's calibre apparently needs. I must admit we get to visit very picturesque places. We hump all this gear to some of the loveliest views in the area. Then Seymour paints and we criticise and we hump it all back with the added burden of a sulky Seymour. The only thing you can say for Seymour's painting is that it leaves the view in the same condition as he found it. An art which is becoming rarer than it ought to be.

above
FARM LANE, WOODSOME

left
GREEN HOUSE LANE, BROWNHILL

*B*luebell time again. It comes round faster every year. It doesn't seem all that long since I became aware of bluebells as a child. There was a bluebell wood I used to play in – with little Tommy Mordew. He was smaller than me, and much more agile. He could go up a tree like a ginger squirrel. Year after year I see the bluebells return but never little Tommy Mordew after that raid over Hamburg in 1943.

GRIMESCAR WOOD

*T*hey say it's been a good lambing season and certainly there's plenty of new life up there. How those young things pluck at the heartstrings. Their play is so like ours used to be. Is it only because we are mammals that we find the young of mammals so beautiful? Few of us get excited about mosquito larvae. Nobody strokes a worm. There are no societies for the prevention of cruelty to bacteria. Except for a few fanatics, slugs are on their own. Prejudice is alive and well and deeply rooted in the species.

HARDEN MOSS

overleaf
HOLME SCHOOL 'PLAYTIME'

'Turned the bend and there was the old school. I like coming across things suddenly. I like them popping up like things from a conjurer's hat.

Long straight roads are efficient but a bit relentless. I like corners – bends. I understand the Romans were great on drains but I'm not sure they had the human touch. Those long straight roads tend to dwarf the aspirations of your average pedestrian. I like the change of scenery that comes as you turn a bend. I like the world coming to me a piece at a time. Changing its shirt regularly.

*O*ld roofs, old stone, old doors, old windows – even the old
Landrover – sit comfortably in their farmyards. Some of
the artifacts of man are able to wear as fittingly into their
surrounds – almost as the earth they rest on or the tree which
shades them.

THUNDERBRIDGE

Wesley took us in his car to a big new supermarket. It was all right but so clean and Space Age we felt like aliens. Old Welly Boots looked distinctly extra-terrestrial in that super nova of groceries. I don't think I'm ready for shopping on that scale. I like shops that fit people – as if they've been made to measure.

right
NETHERTHONG

below
WOOLDALE

overleaf
WESSENDEN MOOR

The hills seem enormous. Such gravity and weight and yet there is, in the machinery of the smallest flower that garlands them, so complex a miracle, so marvellous an intricacy of structure and function that, to the eye of the admirer, the flower becomes as weighty as the hills.

*We passed the pony on the way up. Bonny little creature.
When we arrived up at the higher fields there was the
donkey. 'I've suddenly understood,' Seymour announced,
'what it is about donkeys. They're the Compo Simmonites of
the horse world.'*

above
DONKEY ON CARTWORTH MOOR

right
PONY AT THURSTONLAND

86

'*I like a wild garden,*' *Compo said. '*Just as well,*' *Seymour said. '*You've certainly got one.*' '*I believe in leaving things,*' *Compo added, '*to Mother Nature. She knows best.*' '*Sometimes,*' *Seymour frowned, eyeing the hole in Compo's trousers, '*you can see the handiwork of Mother Nature a mite too clearly round here.*'

right
WINDOW AT UPPER BRIDGE

below
FOXGLOVES, OLDFIELD

*F*ound Wesley supposed to be working on a Morris Minor. He was asleep when we got there – under the car. Of course he denied it. Claimed he was working on the exhaust. We heard him snoring. Sometimes, he told us, working on an exhaust sounds a bit like snoring. I think years of living with Edie have taught Wesley that once he goes for a story he'd better stick to it.

left
RAY GATE, NEW MILL

above
MORRIS MINOR, WOOLDALE

*N*ice to see the hen today free to wander her barnyard. To have the run of the fields. A pinch of inefficiency is a blessing in those who work the land and have the care of creatures.

left
BARN AT HIGHLEY HALL FARM, CLIFTON

below
HAYFIELD, CARTWORTH

We went to the lake. Compo swears there's a fish down there of a size you wouldn't believe. He says you can feel it. We gave it a try. We stood there – trying to feel it. He's right. It feels like a place where you'd find a fish of a size you wouldn't believe.

GUNTHWAITE

We lugged all his stuff until Seymour found a view he wanted to paint. Look at the colours, he ordered. We looked at the colours. Seymour finished his picture. 'Tha's got different colours,' Compo pointed out. 'That's not like Nature's at all.' 'Mine's an improvement,' Seymour said modestly. 'The artist has a licence to improvise.' 'It's time they took thee licence away,' Compo decided.

VIEW FROM TENTER HILL

*B*it dramatic out there this morning. God's lighting man
was working overtime. The earth looked like Toytown.
All the weight seemed to be in the sky.

MOOR NEAR HOLMFIRTH

99

*T*oday the town seemed all steps and sunlight. Not unfittingly, it seemed to me, since we spend our lives for the most part, climbing steps looking for sunlight.

above
FAR BANKS, HONLEY

right
HOLMFIRTH

*S*ometimes I think the great High Street Retail Revolution has passed us by. The Lord be praised. How could you leave your bicycle outside some chainstore megastore? I bet there's no one in Harrod's more pleasant behind a counter than Mrs Glenworthy. There's nobody blasting music in your ears where I go for a pair of trousers. At least I hope not. I haven't been recently. When I say 'recently' I mean like – twenty years. Still I can't imagine Old Tom Shipley going all hi-fi at his age. Fancy buying trousers to the accompaniment of rock music. No wonder the young, these days, can't seem to find anything that fits.

HOLMFIRTH

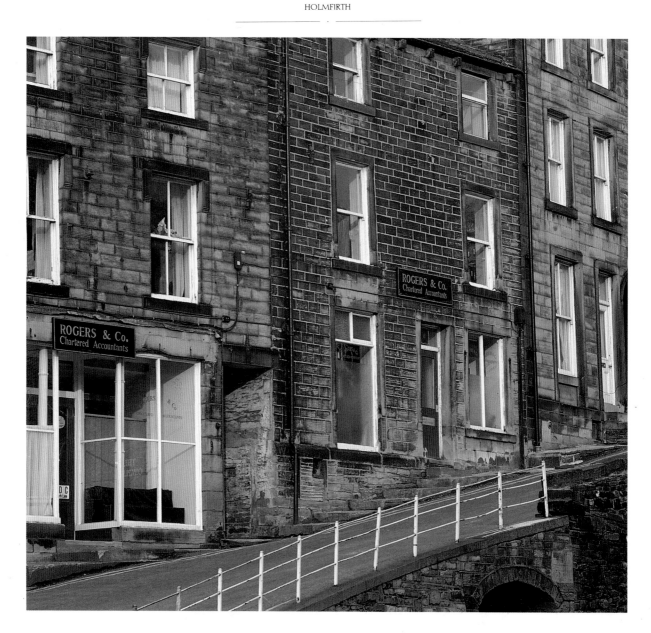

*B*ehind the long shadows and the peace of evening you can almost feel the day slowing down. Settling to its bed – with a countryman's patience – as it has for so many tired but triumphant occasions.

VIEW OF FARNLEY TYAS FROM CASTLE HILL

We wondered how many meals had been cooked on the old range. We decided the place must have been cheerful with a fire burning in the grate while the wind was moaning outside. The old beams looked good for still more years. Compo was becoming impatient with our determination to admire the old place. 'It's a wreck' he said. 'True,' Seymour admitted, 'and if you went home and spent some time on your place you could bring yours up to this standard.'

THURSTONLAND

*S*he has no title deeds but as we passed the old barn this morning, the owner was at her door.

Somebody's relative by marriage, from Wales, was arguing in the pub. I'm constantly amazed at the temerity of people from Wales. This one kept insisting that not only was the natural beauty of his native hills superior to ours, but his home town itself was famous for its parks and corporation grassy areas. Throughout the year, he said, a wealth of colourful blooms. In other words, this was the kind of muffin who could very quickly give you a pain. 'Where's your blaze of colour here in town?' he asked. 'Where is that touch of glory to brighten your streets?' 'On the clothes-lines,' we said. He wore a frown heavy with Welsh incomprehension. Washing we told him. Famed far and wide we are for the quality of our washing. Even our smallest streets have a festive air, especially on Mondays.

right
WASHING ON LINE, MARSDEN

below
DOOR AND CAT, HEPWORTH

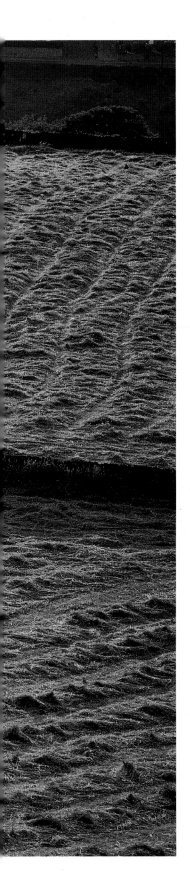

*A*nother year. The harvest in again. A clock that varies little. It was there before the measuring-candle and long before our quartz. And, for this clock, we are the faces on which it marks the passing of the seasons.

left
HAYFIELD, CARTWORTH

below
HAY BALES, LONGLEY

A bonny walk today. The only things we passed were two horses and they paid no attention. I have a fondness for creatures who mind their own business. A little touch of indifference is a great lubricant in any community.

*Y*ou look at views so pleasant you think heaven can't be far
away. Dammit we're on the doorstep.

BRADSHAW

I am pleased continually by reminders of how well our dwellings, hereabouts, have the capacity to merge with the natural world. As if the earth has invested them with its seal of approval.

above
NETHER LANE, BRADSHAW

right
FARM, HOLME

*W*alked a long way today. One of Seymour's instinctive short cuts put about three miles on our journey. For the last hour all I could hear was the small sounds of a welly-booted person expressing displeasure. 'It's not as if we're lost,' Seymour said. 'I know exactly where we are.' 'Knackered,' Compo said. Despite a lack of formal education and even out of breath Compo can be very fluent in languages. At one point the cattle watched us pass. Couldn't help wondering what they were thinking. When you get close you realize they have so much weight and muscle to be putting up with the likes of us. What advantage we take of their gentleness. God in the image of man? We might do better if he was in the image of those patient creatures.

right
COWS ON MEAL HILL, HOLME

below
HIGHLAND CATTLE AT HOLME

I like to see a bit of pride. A touch of caring for places. All the little signs of affection for a dwelling. Houses are like pets. You can tell when they're cherished.

IVY COTTAGE, OLDFIELD

CHAPEL HOUSE FARM, EMLEY

*I*s there anything more dignified than daily tasks being patiently performed? We saw the old lady, her life honoured by work and softened by the sunlight and the flowers round her door.

UPPER BRIDGE, HOLMFIRTH

overleaf
HAYFIELD, LONGLEY

*W*e propped up our bicycles and had a beer in the field. There was a lark rising and somewhere in the distance the drone of a tractor. There was also the remains of somebody's picnic. Sometimes I wish there lived deep in the darkest trees some awesome creature that preyed on litter louts. I dreamed of a rural scene where the bones of litter louts, picked clean, were the only litter.

Passed a farmyard this morning that looked like a farmyard should. With appropriate creatures in their ancient places. What a dignity creatures have in the environments proper to them. Each with enough freedom to be what its nature insists.

SCOUT FARM, MARSDEN

VIEW OF CARTWORTH MOOR

*W*e came over the rise and there was the old car, parked on the high moor. Suddenly it was 1930 again. Our machines date us so. Our stone weathers contentedly and the hills remain wrapped perpetually in their own, unchanging mystery. Only our artifacts bear testimony to the brevity of our lives.

above
NETHER END FARM BUILDINGS

right
CUPWITH HILL

We were hurrying for the pub before it began to rain. There was a bit of wet sunlight leaking from clouds as black and heavy as fruit. 'It'll blow over,' Seymour forecast. Then somebody pulled the plug in the clouds. We squelshed into the pub. The landlord frowned as we dripped onto his carpet. 'He's paying,' Compo said, pointing at Seymour, 'the weather forecaster.'

MELLOR LANE

overleaf
HOLME

Saw a little wooden hut, miles from nowhere. Never mind what it's doing there, how did it get there? Where did they buy it? 'Can you deliver?' they asked. 'No problem,' the salesman said. I hope he had a big sheet of paper when they started giving him the directions. We wondered if they brought it on a lorry from the city. We wondered if they'd found their way home yet.

*T*here used to be dragons in the forests. Now there are chain saws. If St. George is listening I wish he'd take up arms against chain saws. Compo says he doesn't believe there were dragons. And this from a man who lives next door to Nora Batty.

*W*hy is it even the smallest show of water attracts us? Wherever we find it – it draws us. Today we ate our sandwiches with more pleasure, I swear it, because we were sprawled out near water. Afterwards we pottered about its edges until we'd all got our feet wet. The distance between us and being ten years of age was suddenly infinitesimal.

*B*lessedly cool on a hot day is even the voice of water. There are few sounds sweeter. On troubled nights I think it must be easier to sleep within the sound of water. It needn't be anything as momentous as the sea. I haven't the temperament for the enormous. A bit of tumbling water, too small for a name, will do for me.

above
STREAM AT BRADSHAW

left
SUNSET OVER RIVER CALDER

overleaf
VIEW FROM FARNLEY TYAS

The argument this morning was: do you believe life has a purpose? 'We're all monkeys,' Compo said. 'Speak for yourself,' Seymour objected, 'and come down from that tree.' 'I was just demonstrating that we still have the skills.' We helped Little Raggy Britches down from the tree. 'For being a monkey,' Seymour conceded, 'we know very well that you still have the skills.' We walked on. Personally I think things are too beautiful to be entirely accidental. I could be wrong. But not about the beauty.

*U*p close, houses have faces. Just like people. Marks and scars and features. They show the wear and tear of their histories. Then when you switch scale and look at them at a distance, again like people, they tend to gather in groups in a landscape. Small groups of dwellings fit as naturally as people into the scenery. They look as if they belong amid the greenery and under the sky. It's only in cities that they become oppressive, unruly mobs.

right
VIEW OF HINCHCLIFFE MILL

below
WASHING, HINCHCLIFFE MILL

*S*hopping day. Seymour got Compo tidied up a bit. He doesn't mind so much when we're out in the countryside, but when we're in town Seymour tends to walk a few paces in front. He misses nothing; he carries on conversations, but it's a distance which, if he passes someone whom he considers important, enables him to pretend he's not with us. It's the idiosyncrasy of a former headmaster. We don't mind. In fact Compo takes great delight in the game and has a few moves of his own. This morning when Seymour was talking to someone he was trying to impress, Compo sidled nearer. 'This chap with you?' the man asked Seymour. 'The gentleman's not with us,' Compo said, touching his forelock, 'he merely asked us to meet him here so he could donate a pound coin to the good cause we're collecting for.' Seymour coughed, but coughed up. We left. 'Shopping can be fun,' Compo said.

above
IRONMONGERS, HOLMFIRTH

right
VIEW OF HOLMFIRTH FROM CLEGG'S HOUSE

I'm a bit of a moth for lights. Especially when there's a pub behind it. But there's something about the cheerful lights which begin to appear with the coming of darkness. It makes you understand why a creature would go fluttering towards it.

Of course if the stretch of inland water is bigger and has pleasant banks, then the result is as close to heaven as we're likely to get. There's a stretch I know, which on still days with its surface unruffled, stuns the heart into silence. Silence is the respect we owe to places like this, the opportunity to feel the stillness which is the ground and pinnacle of their glory. Even a voice is an intrusion; a power boat an obscenity.

We were looking for a tree. We were in the middle of a wood but we were looking for one tree. Compo's tree. The one he carved his initials on, before the war, when he was going out with Mavis Tunnicliffe. When I say 'going out with' that really means he occasionally used to wrestle Mavis Tunnicliffe, who was well disposed enough to allow him two falls out of three. We spent a full hour looking for his tree. Things change, we told him. Memory is unreliable. It may not have been this part of the wood. It may even have been some other wood. 'Are you sure it was Mavis Tunnicliffe?' we asked him. Turned out to be Audrey Bancroft.

above
WICKINS DIKE, HOLMFIRTH

right
WOOD AND IVY, WOODHEAD ROAD

There are places where earth looks so attractive you could stroke her. She has her coarse furs and her velvets; her muscles and curves and the grace of her flanks. I know of no therapy like landscape for restoring the spirit. There is a companionship possible with this, sometimes wild, often placid creature. The great beast astonishingly patient with us who abuse her.

GIBRIDING LANE

The field was half ploughed. Where it wasn't stubble it looked like plum duff. In fact that fragile slice of rich, nutritious stuff is all that turned a bare planet into Christmas.

above
KNOWL TOP

right
PLOUGHED FIELD, FARNLEY TYAS

Seymour's accent gets two notches posher whenever the hunt goes by. He assumes the air of a man who would himself be wearing a pink coat if only he had the time available. Within the hearing of the huntpersons Seymour gives orders to us in the clipped tones of a leader of the pack. 'Move aside there. Don't startle the horses.' Actually the sight of Compo tends to unnerve the riders more than the horses.

HORSE RIDERS ON WOOD NOOK LANE

As a long time afficionado of the ferret, Compo follows the activities of the hunt with a critical eye. He feels very superior to all the commotion on the grounds that he used to manage with only a ferret and a terrier. 'Not as pretty though, were you.' Seymour pointed out. 'I never had a pink jacket,' Compo admitted. 'I used to have that really cracking, bright green check.' We remembered. He used to wear it with a yellow pullover. We remember it well.

THE HUNT, FARNLEY TYAS

*D*istance. The mind can breathe up here. It's got some place to go. I notice that we three, when we get up high, with just the sky and the miles around us, we grow quieter. If I told them this they'd swear it was because they were tired, but that's not it at all. I think we grow quiet because we are aware of our own smallness. It's an instinctive token of respect.

WESSENDEN HEAD MOOR

*M*ountains are all right for picture postcards. You can't walk them without some desperate struggle with tents, porters, ropes and even oxygen. Our local hills will do for me. Massive enough to be impressive they're still wanderable. All we need is a pair of boots. Even wellies. Not a rope between us, except the one that's holding up the trousers of You-Know-Who.

BRADSHAW

'We could be the Venice of the North.' Who said that? Alderman Percy Trumfleet who, admittedly, was seeking re-election at the time and was, therefore, not unbiased. However, from certain angles, he had a point. For 'gondolier' read 'bargee', and it has to be conceded that our Venice is built upon utility not ornament. But utility has its own graces. Our palaces may be mills but some of them are still making cloth the world recognizes as superior. If we are without ornament we are not without dignity. And dignity is weightier than ornament. Perhaps dignity is our ornament.

HINCHCLIFFE MILL ON FROSTY MORNING

161

*O*ther places have little groups of people huddled together, gossiping. We have houses like that. Our buildings huddle together, staring at each other's windows. Knowing each other's business. There are very few of our dwellings in a position to be standoffish. We are, for the most part, convivial.

HONLEY

overleaf
HOUSE AT WOODSOME

163

Angels don't excite me. I prefer trees. If there's a heaven I shall want oak, hawthorne and ash. And grass. Field after field of grass. And if the buildings are stone I'd like Yorkshire stone. And if there's any room for personal preference (what kind of a heaven would it be without it?) I don't want a climate like Jerusalem thank you. Places need rain. If they've got a good Greens Committee they'll know this already. And harps you can keep. Give me a blackbird.

There were some riders out above the town. We sat on the wall until they passed. They looked sad. Something happens to a person's face when they get on a horse. How often do you see a smiling rider? Except maybe One Tinkle Thompson. And he was on a bike. Rode like a lunatic. Down that long, sloping track from his house – building up speed. Just one tinkle in his bell for emergencies. Long legs, a big grin and a slight deficiency in the bell department. He had to load his bell for every journey. He could use it once then it packed in. Wonder he never got killed. Later we raised a glass in salute to One Tinkle Thompson.

above
HORSE RIDERS ON CARTWORTH MOOR

right
DERELICT FARM, MELTHAM MOOR

We borrowed a boat from Murdock and went out on the lake. Seymour, of course, was in command. Compo was rowing and I was wondering how long it would be before they realized I was doing nothing. It wasn't long. Acidly critical of Compo's performance, Seymour press-ganged me into taking one of the oars. I don't know why it is but the minute I pick up an oar I get water trickling up my sleeve. They say water can't run uphill but it always gets up my sleeve. It was the same that day at Bridlington. We hired a rowboat. The sea, which is supposed to be in the blood of every Englishman, in my case, is always up my sleeve.

WESSENDEN HEAD

Found a painter today. Poor man had climbed with his easel and all his paraphanalia to find this spectacular view. Believed himself alone with Nature then we appeared. Really made his day; especially when Seymour began making suggestions for improving his work. We hauled Seymour away. You have to have sympathy for anyone who sets out to paint around here. Reality has made such a competent job it's a hard act to follow. The natural brushwork round here sets such a frustrating standard. If I were a painter I'd complain bitterly. Seems to me Nature's hogged all the best effects already.

VIEW FROM BUCKSTONE MOSS, SCAMMONDEN

There's a part of me loves these first whiskers of snow and another, older part winces at the thought of winter chills to come. For a second the spirit goes heavily into thermal underwear and dreads the darkness and the electricity bills, and the wind lifting slates. Then you see the first snow decorating workaday roofs – enchanting winter grass and the heart grows reconciled to the turning of another season.

above left
WOOLDALE

above right
NEW MILL DIKE

right
HOLMFIRTH

overleaf
HOLME VILLAGE

The first snow on the tops this morning. Not enough for tobogganing, although Raggy Pants had to try on a piece of plastic the farmers leave about. Seymour was embarrassed by the sight of this unshaven elf cavorting noisily through his mini Winter Olympics. Whenever a car passed us, scattering slush from the road, Seymour strained every sinew to look like someone unconnected with these events. Later, when we dropped down into the village pub, Seymour was even more embarrassed at the steam rising from the soggy garments of our winter sportsman. The landlord wasn't your genial host either.

*S*uperb weather. Compo has a hole in his wellies. With the result that we wander through our archetypal winter wonderland to a running commentary of complaint from guess who. 'Look at the pretty pictures,' we tell him, but beauty, it seems, is not only in the eye of the beholder, but dependent upon the condition of his wellies. Thus it came to pass that we had to abandon fairyland and return home via Wesley's, where Compo was rushed in for repairs. With a puncture repair patch in place, Compo was once more ready for the road, by which time it had clouded over. Goodbye fairyland.

above
VIEW FROM MARK BOTTOMS LANE, HOLMFIRTH

centre
HARDEN MOSS

right
FARM LANE, HOLME

*S*ometimes from that combination of enthusiasm and sheer stupidity which characterizes our wanderings, we go too far. The road home seems endless. It was like that today. Seymour was suffering from an acute attack of leadership and drove us past innumerable pubs into a veritable desert – at one point we walked for an hour and saw only one dwelling perched high on a hill. I think it was Russian. My knees aged twenty years – I'm writing this after a hot bath amid a strong smell of liniment. When we finally arrived home Seymour had a blister. It's the little things that help to restore your faith.

The cat was there again this morning. It came in as I went out for the milk. It's not a stray. It's in good condition. It goes straight to the kitchen and waits for the saucer to be put down. It likes the cream. It doesn't beg. It doesn't make a fuss. It just confers upon me the privilege of feeding it cream. Afterwards it stays for a while and permits me to watch its morning ablutions while I drink my tea. It came out of the blue one Thursday morning and one day I expect it will cease to come. But for the moment we have an understanding. Then off it goes back to its duty and to the high seriousness of being a cat.

left
CAT AT TOTTIES HALL

below
TIRED CAT, HINCHCLIFFE MILL

*G*ot to thinking this morning as we wandered through town about how many feet have worn these stones. There are fossils in stone and there are fossils too of pavement and steps. Traces of the passing of entire generations. The wear and tear of decent, unrecorded lives. Flesh eroding stone.

HOLMFIRTH

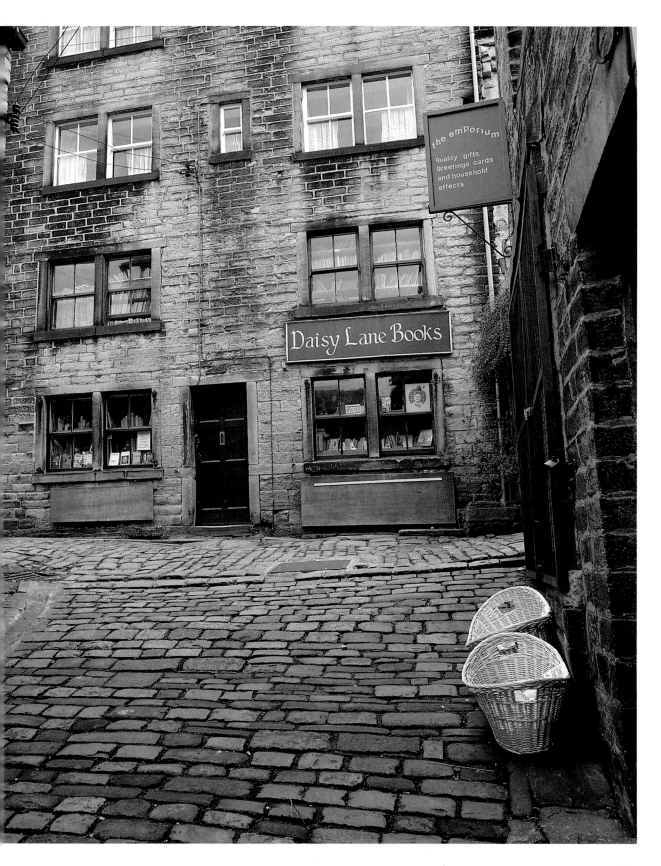

above
DEAN BROOK FARM AT NIGHT

right
SID'S CAFE, HOLMFIRTH

*W*e were out late that day. On our way home we called in
the cafe. It was all dressed up for somebody's party. Its
lights cheerful and self-important with no idea how small
they'd seemed from up there among the evening hills.

At the day's end, when the magnitude of the hills which surround us is fading into the darkness, the town lights its little lights and prepares to navigate the ancient perils of the night.

above
CHIMNEY POTS, CARTWORTH MOOR

right
HOLMFIRTH AT NIGHT

*E*njoyed the snow this morning. It can look so seductive. Then we passed the sheep in a huddle and things went back into perspective. I thought about life's persistent divide of beauty on the one side and need on the other.

As we were passing old Crabtree's place this morning, Seymour decided it looked like a Christmas card. He ordered us to admire it which we thought we'd better do in case he asked us questions on it afterwards. Old Crabtree, who seems to have been Old Crabtree since I was a lad, came round the house corner carrying something in a bucket for the pigs. It smelled delicious. Better than many a bar meal, although Old Crabtree is nobody's idea of a waitress. How old must he be? He looks as old as the stone the house is built of. How many snows must he have known?

above
FARM, SCHOLES

left
HOLME IN SNOW

overleaf
BRADSHAW

It was cold up there today. Wind made your eyes water. We took a long look at the view we'd earned – awesome even through excessive eye fluid – saw the storm coming, bottom heavy, fat clouds bouncing over the hill. On the way down – the wind at our backs, cheeks glowing – anticipating the pub's log fire. Saw the tracks of a hare. How does it navigate, I wonder, all that space and the implacability of winter? I wish it some hare equivalent of the pub's log fire. A respite from hunger, a rest from fear – a necessary death when it comes, from its natural enemies – sooner than the arbitrary feckless whims of man.

For permission to use the extracts from the unpublished journal of Norman Clegg I am indebted, mainly, to a bottle of wine. It wasn't Yorkshire wine, but it was English, from the Isle of Wight actually and very nice too. At any rate, under its softening influence, Clegg was persuaded to relax his rule about keeping his journal private. The result is, I believe, a testimonial to his affection for his native acres and where's the harm in that?

Roy Clarke. Summer 1989.

DRY STONE WALLING, WESSENDEN MOOR

INDEX

DRY STONE WALLING, WESSENDEN MOOR

INDEX